The Mind's Eye
Teacher's Book

The Mind's Eye

Using pictures creatively in language learning

Teacher's Book

Alan Maley, Alan Duff and Françoise Grellet

CAMBRIDGE
UNIVERSITY PRESS

Published by the Press Syndicate of the University of Cambridge
The Pitt Building, Trumpington Street, Cambridge CB2 1RP
40 West 20th Street, New York, NY 10011–4211, USA
10 Stamford Road, Oakleigh, Melbourne 3166, Australia

© Cambridge University Press 1980

First published 1980
Tenth printing 1993

Printed in Great Britain
at the University Press, Cambridge

ISBN 0 521 23333 X Teacher's Book
ISBN 0 521 23332 1 Student's Book

KY

Contents

Acknowledgements

Acknowledgements
The authors and publishers are grateful to those listed below for permission to reproduce illustrations.

Photographs
Coventry Climax Ltd (p. 7); Martin Shallcross (p. 10a and c); Central Office of Information (p. 10b); Paul Hill (p. 10d); John Walsmley (p. 19a); Bob Watkins (p. 19c).
Photographs on pp. 6, 14, 17, 19(b), 24, 27 by Françoise Grellet.
Photographs on pp. 10(e), 15 by Alan Duff.

Painting and drawings
Richard S. Zeisler & Co: *Les Amants* by René Magritte, © ADAGP, Paris 1979 (p. 3); Punch Publications Ltd: cartoons by Graham (p. 12); Christiane Charillon: drawings by Sempé (pp. 21, 22 and 23); Du Mont Buchverlag: tangrams from *Tangram: the ancient Chinese game* by Joost Elffers (Penguin edn) (pp. 25 and 26).
Cartoon on p. 13 by Chris McLeod.

Introduction

When Man Ray, the American surrealist photographer and painter, gave one of his first exhibitions in Paris, he hung some of his works up by a string attached to only one corner. In order to see the picture 'properly', one had to lift it and hold it in the 'right' position. What Ray noticed was that the works hung in this unusual position attracted far more attention than his conventionally hung pictures. This was not just a stunt. He was asking the viewer to make a small personal effort, to stop and look at the work not as an exhibit but as a picture.

A similar attempt to break down the barrier between the viewer and the work has been launched in the Paris métro: pictures are hung along the walls of the underground tunnel, to be glimpsed in the flashing light of the passing train. Sculptors, too, have designed works which are set in motion by pressing a pedal or pulling a string, or statues that can be climbed into, onto, over and through.

A picture is wordless. It does not, like a text, tell us what its 'meaning' is. What we see in a picture depends as much on what we are as on what it is.

In this book, we try to do what Man Ray did – hang the pictures up by one corner to be looked at more carefully. We try, like the artists in the métro, to look at pictures outside their usual context, to explore their wordlessness.

Paradoxically, perhaps, it is because pictures say nothing in words that so much can be said in words about them. And this is why they can be so effectively used in language learning. For, unlike texts, they do not require to be understood, dissected, summarised or explained. A picture is open to interpretation, and this is why the book is called *The Mind's Eye*, because it is concerned with what the mind *sees*.

How the book can be used

The Mind's Eye is intended for language learners – mother tongue and foreign language alike – who need, and want, language practice. The skills of speaking and writing are developed.

Most of the exercises will be done in small groups, usually in pairs, but it is extremely important that these groups or pairs should not be static. The exercises are so designed that whatever is produced in the smaller groups should be later communicated to others in the class. This exchange of information and impressions is essential because it is at this stage that the learner comes to re-express ideas in the face of opposition, disagreement, scepticism or, perhaps, enthusiasm.

Level

Whenever stimulating language material is produced, the immediate question is always: 'Yes, but at what *level* can it be used?' This is, perhaps, reasonable in discussing written material, in which one can certainly distinguish levels of complexity and difficulty. But with non-verbal material (pictures, sounds, mime, etc.) the question is inappropriate. The level is determined by the *user*, not by the material. There are no difficult or easy pictures. Nor do pictures 'illustrate' styles and registers

1

(colloquial, idiomatic, literary, scientific, etc.). In principle, then, this material can be used from the very early learning stage, and with most age groups, from early secondary school onwards.

What matters, in using pictures, is not defining a level but – almost the opposite – ridding oneself of ready-made ideas as to what the learners can or cannot do. To speak of a group or class of thirty individuals as 'they' or 'my class' is as dangerous as speaking of *the* Russians or *the* English. One may generally be right in predicting what learners can do, but this can never be more than an assumption based on experience. In devising this material, therefore, we have tried to make no unnecessary prior assumptions.

As a result, you will find that some apparently bizarre demands are being made in the exercises. We suggest, for instance, that short poems be written (by people who may never even have read a poem in the target language before!), that film scripts be compiled, that advertisements be invented, that book titles or newspaper headlines be provided. Why not? It should not be assumed in advance that, simply because someone has never before tried his hand at writing a film script, he must be incapable of doing so.

In short, we are suggesting that the learner be given the opportunity to find out for himself what he can or cannot do.

How the book is organised

The Mind's Eye is designed for use in class. The Student's Book is made up of pictures and corresponding exercises, divided into fifteen sections, each of which illustrates a certain type of picture. The Teacher's Book contains detailed information on sixteen techniques which can be used with different types of picture, and it provides further useful information on the pictures and exercises in each section of the Student's Book.

The sections are composed as follows:

Main picture

This is a full-page picture at the beginning of each section in the Student's Book. Through the exercises in the Student's Book and the suggestions in the Teacher's Book on which techniques are suitable, it is studied in detail illustrating the kind of treatment that could be given to other pictures in the section.

Additional examples

In most sections two half-page pictures belonging to the same category follow the main picture. The most interesting features of the picture are brought out by questions, and there are suggestions for follow-up work relating to the picture.

Pictures without comment

The end of the section usually contains a double-page spread of four pictures. These are intended to show the type of picture that might be used (for it is assumed that users of the book will also do their own collecting). Reference will often be made to these pages in exercises such as 'building a story out of pictures', in which we suggest that a particular picture be combined with any four or five others in the book.

Techniques

We use the word 'techniques', but this should not imply that the suggestions must be carried out to the letter! These are not instructions for operating a washing machine; they are methods that have grown up, through trial and error, through experiment and constant change. And no doubt they will continue to change. However, for those who are not used to working with pictures, or who have not had the opportunity to develop their preliminary experiments, they should offer a useful and easy-to-follow introduction to this almost limitless material. And those who are already using pictures regularly may be stimulated to see fresh openings and new combinations.

The word 'combination' is important here, because it is often possible to use different techniques with the same picture. Indeed, it is by combining techniques that one discovers how versatile a single image can be. Each picture is open to exploitation with a number of different techniques. No picture should be set aside as having been 'done' simply because it has served for one technique. In addition we have found that pictures reveal an astonishing versatility when set alongside other pictures in novel re-combinations.

1 Guessing the picture

Choice of pictures

This technique requires careful selection of the pictures. Ideally, the picture should:
– contain little detail.
– have a strong focal point (i.e. the eye should be attracted to one spot).
– involve at least one unusual detail.
This means that landscapes, crowded street scenes, 'fussy' interiors, and 'straight' portraits are generally unsuitable. Cartoons and pictures of works of art can occasionally be used, e.g. some of the lesser-known works of Magritte.

(Richard S. Zeisler Collection, New York)

What to do

Initially, this should be done as an exercise involving the whole group or class.

One person holds the picture so that only he or she can see it. The others must try to 'reconstruct' the picture as accurately as possible by asking questions to which the answer will be 'Yes/No', or 'Maybe/Not quite/Almost', etc. It may seem to be stating the obvious to say that both the questions and the answers must be *precise*; experience shows, however, that they often are not. Questions, for instance, such as: 'Is it big?' 'Is it beautiful?' 'Is he or she doing something?' are purely relative. And answers such as: 'I suppose so', 'It's hard to say', etc. are of little or no help.

The pattern of question and answer in this technique can be predicted with fair accuracy. There are certain strategies, therefore, that the picture-holder should bear in mind if the exercise is to succeed. To start with, the questioners will usually try to establish where the picture is set, if there are any people or animals visible, and, if so, how many.

e.g. Is it inside?
Is it outside?
Is it a landscape?
Are there any people in the picture?
Are there any animals?
Is it a nice day?
Are there many people?

It is quite possible to answer all these questions – and they are typical questions – with 'Yes' or 'No'. But the person answering the questions should encourage greater precision from his questioners. He can do this, for instance, by tossing the question back, e.g. 'Is it inside?' – 'Inside what?' This is not unreasonable, because the picture may contain both an interior and an exterior, or it may be taken underwater! Likewise, the question 'Is it a landscape?' is a vague way of saying 'Are there cows, trees and daffodils ... and that sort of thing?' The person answering might turn this question by saying, 'What is a landscape?' or (more provocatively) 'If you mean "Is it a ploughed field?", the answer's No.' Questions about 'many people' and 'a nice day' are both relative, and should not be answered until they are put more precisely.

Once these details have been cleared up, the questions will centre on either an action being performed (Is he sitting? Sawing? Swimming? etc.) or a question of detail (Is she wearing a skirt? A ballroom-dress? A bikini? etc.). These lists of questions can go on indefinitely if the person answering does not attempt to persuade his questioners to change tack. He may do this by saying, 'It's not important' (if this is true) or by suggesting that they try to find questions which will reduce the range of possibilities more rapidly. For instance, in using an advertisement showing a man leaping up out of the ocean (to the astonishment of an admiring dolphin), one will have to answer 'No' to all questions such as: 'Is he standing?' 'Is he sitting?' etc. Questions such as: 'Are his feet on the ground?' or 'Is his body being lifted by anyone?' might get the questioners out of their cul-de-sac.

A final point: intonation. Whoever answers the questions should be careful to stress words which it is important to understand correctly.

e.g. 'Are they eating?
They aren't eating ... *or* They aren't *eating* ...

This should be used sparingly, for, although it stimulates interest quickly, the interest lags noticeably after twenty minutes.

The technique is best used with large groups, of ten or more, though it may occasionally be tried as a warming-up exercise to technique 2, *Reconstructing the picture*.

2 Reconstructing the picture

Choice of pictures

Use pictures with a strong focal point, as in technique 1, *Guessing the picture*, but with more surrounding detail.

What to do

This exercise is best done in groups of four, two pairs working together. Each pair is given a picture and told to study it closely for detail, but not to try and interpret it. Only limited time should be allowed (about three minutes). The pairs in each group now exchange pictures. Each pair in turn attempts to 'reconstruct' its own picture, which is in the hands of the other pair (pair A), who should avoid saying whether the details given are correct or not. For example, if pair B says:
    'The man's standing in mud up to his knees . . .'
pair A would not say:
    'No, he isn't.'
They might, however, *hint* that this is not accurate by asking:
    'Up to his *knees* . . .?'
Once pair B have 'exhausted' their picture, pair A might prod their memories with more direct questions such as:
    'Was there anything round the man's neck?'
or
    'Was anything written on the lifebelt?'
Before fatigue sets in, the picture should be revealed, examined and discussed. Since the *language of discussion* enters into many of these techniques, it is worth recalling here some of the phrases that will typically be needed:

You/we forgot (the dog, the smoke, etc.)
You said her (scarf) was (green), but it's (red).
You/we didn't mention (the screwdriver).
You see, he wasn't (kneeling), he was (crouching).
But I'm sure we mentioned that!
No, what you said was . . . (there's a patch of oil on the *sand*), you didn't mention . . . (the *towel*.)

One should also remember that there will be *disagreement* between the partners as they try to reconstruct their picture:

I'm sure the (tatoo) was (on his *right* arm).
I don't think so/I don't think it was . . .
No, *she* wasn't (holding the umbrella). *He* was.
The (dog) wasn't (on a lead). It was (on a chain).
I still think (it was a lead).

3 You're a witness

Here, we are relying on the same skill as that needed in technique 2, *Reconstructing the picture* – accuracy of recollection.

Choice of pictures
In selecting the pictures, one is looking particularly for:
– scenes of action and movement, preferably involving several people.
– pictures with several focal points and numerous details.

What to do

Divide the class into groups of four, two pairs in each group. Give each group two pictures to study. A strict time-limit should be imposed, in which each pair must look at both pictures. When the time is up, the pictures are turned face down, and the two pairs note down independently the details they have retained. Once again, a time-limit (about five minutes) should be imposed. Each group of four now joins another, to make a group of eight. Pictures are exchanged. The two pairs in group A now 'cross-question' Group B about what they witnessed in their pictures. The two pairs in Group B will reply 'together', but as they are working from *two* sets of notes, there are likely to be discrepancies in their accounts! In this technique, the examining group is more active than in 2, *Reconstructing the picture*. They will be looking for the inconsistencies and also trying to confuse the witnesses. (They might ask about details which were *not* in the picture, e.g. '. . . and where was the motorbike parked?' even though there was no motorbike.)

The same technique can be used particularly well with slides. The slides are shown to the group as a whole, who then break into smaller groups of three or four for the recall. Before the slides are shown again, the groups should discuss their notes, paying special attention to points of disagreement.

4 Speculation

One of the main difficulties in the preceding techniques is that there is a natural temptation to skip the phase of observation and to move straight on to 'interpretation'. If the first three techniques are to work well, the discussion must be strictly focused on the *observable*, and students should be restrained from leaping to interpretations.

In what we call 'speculation' however, (which we prefer to 'interpretation' because it does not imply that there is a *single* interpretation), the observer lets his mind run freely over the picture. To put it very simply, he is asking himself, 'What could be going on here, then? It might be this . . . It might be that.'

Choice of pictures

Clearly, pictures which do *not* lend themselves readily to interpretation are the most suitable. But seemingly straightforward pictures (such as the one of the man in the laboratory on p. 9 in the Student's Book) should not be excluded. What one is looking for, then, are pictures which:

- involve actions, people or objects that could be *outside* the frame.
- involve actions that cannot be conclusively 'explained' or identified.
- involve incidents that have *already happened* or are *about to happen*.
- show people who in some way stand out from their surroundings (such as the portrait of the young man on p. 6 in the Student's Book), whose expressions are ambivalent or mystifying, or else suggestive of an emotional state (anger, joy, etc.) for which no cause can be found in the picture.
- contain mysterious objects, people or scenes.

In short, anything that is puzzling, baffling, mysterious, shocking, amusing, or intriguing is likely to be suitable. Even advertisements that may appear at first to be self-explanatory can also be used, either by removing the caption or by cutting off some part of the picture.

What to do

Exercises in speculation can be conducted in many different ways. Here are some of the most common:

a) Divide the class into pairs. Each pair is given a picture to examine and discuss. In speculating, they attempt not only to explain what is happening, but also *who* the people involved are, *how* they came to be there, *what* has just happened or is going to happen, etc. They can then either:
   - write down in note form the conclusions they came to, then pass on the picture to another group. *Or*
   - break up (one partner staying behind with the picture, and the other moving on to someone else). The person who has moved will now try to find out what his new partner thought of the picture he was working on. They will then discuss the picture together; the newcomer will remain behind with the picture, so that his partner can move on. Thus constant exchange of partners and pictures takes place.

b) If all groups are working with the *same* picture (as they could, using this book), it is possible to ask them all to speculate on the same question(s). In a picture involving people, you might ask them to suggest the dialogue which is taking place or has taken place; in a picture involving action, you might ask them to discuss the background to the events and their possible outcome.

Speculation enters, in fact, into all but the first three techniques in this book. Beginners (not in language but in the use of pictures), often complain that they 'don't know what the picture is *about*' or that they 'have no imagination'. The best way of helping them to see that they don't *need* to know what the picture is about, and that is not so much imagination that is required as patience and willingness to reason, is t suggest that at first they try to answer certain specific questions. These questions car be asked of nearly all pictures, and their purpose is not to provide answers but to set speculation in motion. They are:

For people
- How old might he/she be?
- What is his/her profession?
- Do his/her clothes indicate anything about: profession, job, income, status, nationality, temperament, etc.?
- What does he/she like doing? (e.g. eating, drinking, etc.)
- Is he/she married?
- What is he/she feeling at this moment?

For interior/exterior scenes
- What time of day is it?
- What is the weather like? How can you tell?
- What lies outside the frame of the picture? (i.e. If we are looking at a room, what sort of building is it in? If a landscape, what lies over the horizon, behind the hills, etc?)
- Are there any signs of the presence of people or animals? (e.g. hat on chair, dog's basket etc.)

For events/actions
- Can we *see* the cause of this event in the picture?
- If the event has already taken place, how long ago did it happen? If it has not yet taken place, when will it occur?
- Are there any other people, machines, objects, etc. involved that cannot be seen in the picture?

In answering these questions, the students will begin to realise how much is taken for granted (and wrongly so) by the mind's eye. The more closely one examines a picture, the richer speculation becomes.

5 Linking pictures

This technique should always be preceded by at least one warming-up exercise in observation or speculation, as it is one which draws on the ability to 'see into' a picture and, most important, to *think beyond the frame*.

Choice of pictures

In principle, 'anything goes'. In practice, however, it is preferable to make a selection. Different pictures containing a common element (e.g. a piano, a giraffe, two people arguing, etc.) are particularly suitable. Variety, too, is important. As each group will be working with a set of five or six pictures, one must ensure that there is a balance between pictures containing several people and those with none, between black-and-white and coloured pictures, and between abstract and figurative images. There should also be a balance between ambiguous and unambiguous pictures. (Note that this technique is easier to handle with loose pictures cut from magazines.)

What to do

The class should be divided into groups of four to six. Each group is given the same number of pictures. The purpose is to develop a story featuring each of the pictures. The pictures are linked by narration, and the group has the right to move freely across the barriers of time, i.e. some pictures may represent time past, others time present or time to come.

About ten minutes should be allowed for preparation. When a group is ready, all but two people go to other groups. As groups work at different speeds, those who finish soonest will move to any other group that also happens to be ready. The newcomers now attach themselves to a pair with a different set of pictures. These pictures are laid out *in the order in which they appear in the story*. The task of the newcomers is to work out the story by looking at the pictures and questioning the pair who know the story. They must offer, rather than ask for, explanations. Thus a typical exchange would be:

A: This woman is recalling her past, isn't she?
B: Not exactly recalling ...
A: She's dreaming, then?
B: Yes ...
A: And in her dream, she travels to South America?
B: Yes, but who with?
A: With this man?
B: No ... you see, it's only partly a dream ...

This is a most stimulating exercise, and less difficult than it may seem. It has several great advantages: it enables the students to re-use pictures they may have worked on in earlier techniques, giving them a new dimension by setting them in an entirely different context; it allows for free play of the imagination – but not wasted imagination – since the ideas that are produced will later be discussed.

There is usually no need to control the movement of the groups. Their own interest will carry them from one set of pictures to another.

6 Linking cartoons

In this technique, different cartoons are linked to form a sequence. As in 5, *Linking pictures* the students are asked to think 'beyond the frame' and to imagine in what possible ways the pictures might be related.

Choice of pictures

Any sequence of three, four or five cartoons will do, provided they have no caption or you leave the caption out. Try to select cartoons that are drawn in a clear way and not too difficult to understand.

You can vary this by choosing drawings by the same cartoonist. The characters often look very similar, so the students may believe that the same person appears in two or three of the drawings. This may give rise to totally different kinds of stories. (Note that this technique is easier to handle with loose cartoons cut out from newspapers or magazines.)

What to do

Divide the class into groups of four or five and give a different set of cartoons to each group. Allow them about ten minutes to work out a story that will link the cartoons. They can arrange the drawings in any order they like and think of them as referring to past, present or future time, as they wish.

When a group has finished, they should go to another group which is also ready and tell them their story. This new group will then ask them further questions to get more details about the story, the characters, their reasons for behaving as they did, etc. They may also try to find weak points in the story they have heard. Here are some of the phrases they may need:

You've just said that . . ., but . . .

But if she is . . ., then how can you explain that . . .?

It can't possibly be . . .

I can't see how she could possibly . . . since . . .

It wasn't a . . ., you said it was a . . .

When they have finished, the second group will tell their story in their turn.

It is also possible to use the procedure described in 5, *Linking pictures*.

7 Filling the gap/Finding the last picture

For these two techniques, a series of pictures or cartoons is used. Some elements in this series (either the beginning, the middle or the end) are hidden and the students are asked to work out the missing link. It is mainly an exercise in imagination and it is a good test of the students' ability to think 'laterally' and to find unexpected links in stories which too often develop in an obvious way.

Choice of pictures

Almost any sequence can be used for *Finding the last picture*, since it is usually in the last picture that the unexpected twist that makes the story interesting, unusual or amusing appears. For *Filling the gap*, it is essential to find a series of pictures in which the missing element will create a mystery or a problem. In the following sequence, for instance, the students have to work out what might have happened in between the first three pictures and the last two of the series to account for the complete change in the man's behaviour.

What to do

Divide the class into groups of two or three and give them all the same picture story, asking them to supply the end or the missing elements. Set a time-limit (no more than ten minutes). Then the groups can work in different ways:

a) Each group can be asked to sum up their version of the story in one sentence – no more. A piece of paper is passed round the class, each group writing their sentence down, then folding the paper so that the next group cannot see what has been written. When everyone has finished, the paper is unfolded and the different interpretations read out. This is a good way of forcing the students to be concise and to say what they think in a limited number of words.

b) Another possibility is for each group to join another group who will try to discover their interpretation by asking 'twenty questions'. This is not as difficult as it may sound since they have already been thinking about the same series of pictures and have some idea of what the possibilities could be. Students will soon discover that general questions will be more effective than very precise ones and will quickly narrow down the field of possibilities.

8 Blurred focus

This technique is best used with slides since it is very easy when using a projector not to focus the slide at once, but to do so little by little in three or four steps. This is an interesting technique to make one conscious of the shape of things, of how similar two very different things might be, things one would never have thought of associating but which, through the use of this slow focusing process, have both seemed likely interpretations at one stage.

Choice of pictures

Virtually any picture can lend itself to this type of use.

What to do

First show a completely out-of-focus picture. As a class or in groups, the students speculate on what it looks like, what it could be, etc. They should be encouraged, not only to give a global interpretation but also to try to explain details in the picture (e.g. 'I suppose that thing in the corner might be a . . .', 'And that dark area is probably the shadow . . .').

By turning the lens of the projector, bring the picture a little more into focus, while still leaving it fairly blurred. This can be done two or three times before the picture is shown in focus.

When trying to think of possible interpretations, the students will obviously need to express degrees of probability, using phrases such as the following:
I suppose it is . . .
It might/could/may be . . .
Perhaps it is . . .

Whenever the picture becomes clearer, they will often have to change their former interpretations and phrases such as the following will be useful to them:
Then it wasn't a . . .
That can't be a . . .
This is too . . . to be a . . .
It looks more like a . . .

This technique lends itself particularly well to written work. Working individually or in groups, the students can be asked to produce short poems, captions, headlines, titles of books, etc. inspired by the pictures.

9 Who am I?

This technique is closely related to the pictures in section 1, 'Portraits'. The main aim here is to identify as closely as possible with the person(s) represented in the picture.

Choice of pictures

Portraits will be needed. There are no restrictions on the kind of portrait used, except that it is advisable to avoid pictures of well-known personalities.

What to do

Various approaches are possible:
a) The students work in pairs. Each pair is given a portrait. The members of each pair then discuss the portrait, building up as clear as possible a picture of his or her personality. For guideline questions see 4, *Speculation*. Once they have built up their study of the character they either:
    – pass the picture on to another pair, after first having noted down their impressions. *Or*
    – separate, one person staying behind with the picture, the other moving on to sit with someone else. The new pairs now compare impressions of the portrait.
b) Using the portraits on pp. 6–11 of the Student's Book, the whole group can participate in a guessing game. For this, a tape-recording of different voices, men's and women's, will be needed. Each voice should be heard saying a few sentences. The students will then try to match the voices with the portraits. The purpose of the exercise is to explore the preconceptions we have of a person's physical appearance when we can hear but not see that person as, for instance, on the telephone.

c) Matching portraits is a similar activity. Here, a large range of very different pictures is needed. The students, working in pairs, are asked to find a 'partner' for each person. These need not necessarily be man–woman relationships, but in each case they must specify what the relation is, e.g. father–son, builder–mate, husband–ex-wife, etc. Since this exercise involves making assumptions about personality on the basis of only the portrait, it is advisable to practise technique a) before moving on to this more demanding variant.

d) *Interviews*

This is a fairly complex exercise and will require some preparation. However, as it leads to the kind of language that occurs in role-play exercises, it is well worth the trouble. Before distributing or showing the portraits, give the students some examples of interviews in the target language. For those whose target language is English, an excellent source can be found in magazines, in which the style of the interview is generally informal. Here are two extracts from the *Sunday Times* feature 'A Life in the Day of ...' (The particular advantage of these interviews is that the questions are *not* given; the students can therefore be asked to deduce what questions must have been put to obtain the information.)

Desmond Morris
'On a writing day, crack of dawn for me is between 10 and 11. I'm an owl rather than a lark. My brain is lousy in the morning, improves during the day and reaches peak efficiency round midnight. That's why my intense spells of writing are between 10 p.m. and 4 a.m. I like a light breakfast, tea and toast ... Then I'll go for a swim.'

Jimmy Reid
'My work starts at the Marathon Yard at half-past seven, so I set the alarm for about half-past six. Usually I'm up and dressed by then. Always on my own, though; the wife and kids don't have to go out until later, so I see no point in waking them. There used to be a tradition in working-class homes that the woman got up to make a man's breakfast and see him out. But not now; I wouldn't have that.'

First, discuss the way in which personalities come out in an interview. What tactics, for instance, do people use to avoid awkward questions? Then, distribute a portrait to each person. (If they are working from this book, they can select any person they like.)
The instructions given are: You are this person, and you are well-known. A journalist from a provincial newspaper is coming to interview you. Decide: Who you are, what sort of person you are, how you talk, etc. And, of course, why you are famous.
It helps if students work in pairs, as they often experience difficulty in getting into someone else's skin. A partner will often help by commenting on ideas and offering suggestions. Once the characters have been established, but *only then*, tell the group that each person will be both an interviewer and an interviewee. They now have four minutes, no more, to prepare rough questionnaires for the interviews they are about to hold. Now, each person should choose a partner (not the one he has been working with): each will in turn interview and be interviewed. The interviewer, it should be added, is a 'green' journalist, who does not know as much as he or she should about the famous person to be interviewed. This means

that the interviewer will constantly be trying to extract information that he or she ought to know, and the famous person will be (wrongly) assuming that no explanations are needed for his remarks. The interview should be allowed to run its course without any outside pressure. Once the interviewer is satisfied, he should be shown the *portrait* of the person he was talking to.

If time permits, the exercise should be repeated with a different partner. The second interview usually runs more smoothly as the students have grown to 'know' themselves. And the change of questioner ensures that monotony does not set in.

An interesting extension to this exercise is for each pair to record an interview, preferably the second, so that it can be played back for comment.

10 Finding the words

This is a technique which can be used in almost all sections. It involves written work based on the stimulus of a picture.

Choice of pictures

Almost completely open.

Pictures as illustrations

With a little imagination, it is possible to see almost any picture as if it were, for instance, the photograph on the cover of a book or on a record sleeve, a photograph accompanying an article or news report, a family snapshot, a 'still' from a film, an illustration from a biography, etc. Notice how the following picture 'changes' if one tries to imagine it as any of these.

Even abstract designs, such as this one can be used.

And, after the initial surprise is overcome, the simplest of all 'pictures', a mere square of colour, will often prove to be more stimulating than the apparently 'interesting' pictures.

What to do

There are various possibilities:

a) The students should work in pairs or groups of three. Each group is given a picture. The instructions should be limited to three different requirements *at most*, for instance: Imagine this is i) an advertisement, ii) a book cover, and iii) a press or magazine photograph. Write down the advertising slogan, the title of the book, and the headline of the article accompanying the picture.

 The students should be urged not to become too philosophical or to attempt to be funny at all costs. Each picture is handed out with a large sheet of paper. The students write their ideas down, fold the paper over so that the writing cannot be read, then pass the picture together with the sheet on to another pair. Like this, the pictures circulate freely (it is advisable to have one or two extra ones, since some will get temporarily 'blocked'); at the end, the papers are unfolded and the various suggestions read out aloud.

 Although the written product may seem slight, it is in fact extremely rich. It should not be forgotten that before writing anything down, the students will discuss several possibilities. They will, moreover, be attempting to express themselves as concisely as possible. It is interesting to note that this exercise often brings out metaphors, figures of speech, allusions to contemporary events, etc., that are not given a chance to emerge in routine language work. A blue square, for instance, yielded: 'The sky's the limit', 'New "masterpiece" at the Tate', 'On a clear day you can see forever', and 'French future, as seen by Raymond Barre'!

b) In many sections, we suggest that students write film or play scripts, poems, fragments from diaries, etc. Once they get used to writing, and to having their writing read by others, they will appreciate this outlet for further reflection on the pictures. It may, however, help to give them examples of the kind of language expected.*

c) *Dialogue*

The pictures that can be used for dialogue production will generally, but not always, involve two or more people.

This can be done similarly to technique a), by passing the picture round, with a sheet of folded paper (which ensures that the dialogue exchanges are kept short). An interesting variant is for each pair to select, without announcing their choice, a picture from a set of eight to ten displayed on the wall. They then write a very short exchange, or even a single sentence, to match their picture. These mini-dialogues are then read aloud; the others must guess which picture is being referred to. (This technique is best used with smallish groups of up to eight pairs.)

* See Michael Swan: *Kaleidoscope, Spectrum;* Alan Maley and Alan Duff: *Words!;* Alan Duff: *That's Life!;* Susan Morris: *Love* (Cambridge University Press).

d) *Longer writing exercises*

In 5, *Linking pictures*, we described how story-chains could be produced orally by linking a set of five or six pictures. This same exercise can be extended in writing. The advantage of the written work is that it gives each individual the opportunity to try out ideas he or she may not have been able to express during the group work.

11   Ordering a sequence

This is an exercise which gives practice in a skill that is often ignored in language learning: the ability to classify and arrange. This ability directly involves the notions of expressing similarity and difference, logical sequence and consequence (e.g. 'This one comes next, because . . .', 'That couldn't go there, because if it did . . .').

Choice of pictures

Abstract drawings, designs, geometric patterns, and all non-figurative pictures are particularly suitable. Likewise, figurative pictures containing a common element (e.g. a tree, a certain colour or shape, etc.) will be useful. You can also use pictures which already belong to or form a sequence, and are here presented out of order.

What to do

There are various possibilities:

a) *Pattern sequences*

An interesting way of producing your own material for this exercise is to play an extract of music and ask the students to produce visual impressions of what they hear. These 'drawings' are then collected and redistributed to the students, working in groups of four. Ideally, each group should have at least eight pictures to arrange, so it may be necessary to get them to do two drawings each. Each group then arranges the drawings in accordance with their own criteria of classification, which might be, for instance, straight-line patterns, followed by curved patterns, followed by mixed patterns. Inevitably, most groups will have one or two pictures which do not fit their sequences. If they wish, they may try to exchange the 'misfits' with other groups – but they must keep the same number of pictures. When they are ready, three members of the group move to another group, where they should try to discover the principle on which the sequence of pictures is based.

b) *Broken sequences*

Sets of pictures, such as those found in documentary articles in illustrated magazines, illustrations from technical handbooks and manuals, cartoon strips, etc. can be used. Each set is cut up into separate pieces (if possible, the same number to each set). The pieces are then mixed. Divide the class into as many groups as there are sets of pictures (i.e. if there are eight sets of pictures, there should be eight groups). Each group receives a mixed set of pictures. Their task is to collect *one* set. Once they have decided which set to try for they conceal all the pictures belonging to other sets, so that only they can see them.

Each group must now send round a bargainer, to try to obtain the missing pieces from the other groups. But, in order to do so, he or she must: i) describe as closely as possible the piece that is needed (this means that the groups have to do a considerable amount of collective guessing, particularly in the early stages, to help the bargainer); ii) have a picture that can be offered in exchange.

The ostensible purpose of the exercise is for one group to complete its set first, but the real purpose is to provide an exercise which will involve collective discussion, bargaining, reasoning, and scheming (see also 13, *Jigsaws*).

c) *Cartoons*

For this technique any good sequence of three to six drawings can be used but the best are certainly those in which there is not too much difference between the pictures in the series.

You can use the same series of pictures for the whole class. Divide the class into groups so that in each group there will be one picture for two students. There should be no indication whatsoever of the order in which the pictures appear. The students should be allowed five to ten minutes to look at their drawing and speculate on what it means, and particularly to try to guess what might have happened just before and what will take place immediately afterwards. Then, in each group, the first pair to be ready will tell the others what is in their picture and what they think might come before or after. The other pairs will then describe their own drawings and after asking questions, checking details, etc. the group should agree on a sequence.

When all the groups have finished, each group explains and defends their story and the others try to find weak points in it.

Obviously, sequences in which a different ordering of the pictures is possible are ideal. Otherwise, the second part of the exercise will simply have to be left out.

When doing this exercise, the students will constantly need to use adverbs of time and link-words:

e.g. Then it must be before yours.

　　You said the car was O.K. on your picture? So ours must come afterwards.

　　It can't be much later because . . .

12 Split Cartoons

The aim of this technique is to get the students to reconstruct a cartoon little by little, showing only one element of the picture at a time and asking for comments at each stage. It is an interesting way of realising what different meanings things can take on when they are drawn out of their context. Even when one has all the elements of a picture, there can still be many possible ways of organising them.

Choice of pictures

It is better to use cartoons without a caption and in which there are a certain number of interrelated elements. For instance, a cartoon just showing a lot of people at a party might be amusing because of their expressions or of the way they are dressed, but would probably not lend itself well to this technique.

It is possible to use large-scale pictures that have been enlarged and are shown to the class. However this technique is most easily handled using a slide projector or overhead projector. Here is, for instance, a possible way of splitting a cartoon:

 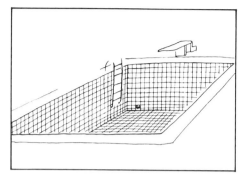

What to do

This is probably best done as a class exercise, although there will be group work at each stage. Divide the class into groups of three or four and project the first slide. Each group should agree on an interpretation of what they can see and also build up a whole scene 'beyond the frame'. For instance, in the case of picture 1, if they think that the top floor is flooded, they should decide what happened exactly, why, where the owners are, why the water didn't run downstairs, etc.

The next slides are then projected, one after the other, and the groups should try to explain each new element so that it will fit in with their first interpretation. This usually makes for a greater variety of stories as there will be a certain amount of 'competition' between groups, each trying to show that their theory was quite good and can very well account for the new details of the cartoon that are shown.

13 Jigsaws

The idea of the jigsaw will be familiar to many from childhood. A picture is pasted to firm cardboard, photocopied (if possible), then cut up into small irregular pieces.

Choice of pictures

Most pictures can be used, but the best are usually those which contain a balanced mixture of detail and open expanses.

It is easier to make your own jigsaws by using pictures from magazines and cutting them into pieces. The following illustrations show how it is possible to cut a picture so that its various elements will not be easily recognisable, therefore requiring careful questioning on the part of the students to reconstruct the original picture.

What to do

There are various possibilities:
a) Using one jigsaw picture only (with smaller classes), distribute a single piece to each person. The picture should be reconstructed on a felt board or on any surface to which the pictures can be attached. It is built up by the students 'offering' their

pieces verbally, i.e. they must describe what is on their piece and where they think it fits. They then try to fit it into the appropriate place.

The following expressions are likely to be needed:

My piece goes in the top corner.

I've got a corner piece.

Mine goes next to yours.

Mine should fit next to the red one.

b) Prepare one jigsaw for each group. Each jigsaw is cut up into the *same number* of pieces. These pieces are then mixed and distributed to the groups. Each group receives the same number of pieces. The task is to reconstruct a picture, and the same procedure is followed as was described on p. 20, 11b, *Broken sequences:* i.e. in order to obtain a piece from another group, the bargainer must: i) be able to describe with reasonable accuracy what he or she requires; ii) have a piece to offer in exchange.

c) Another way of using jigsaws is to follow the procedure described on p. 21, 11c, *Cartoons.* Each pair in the group has a few pieces of the jigsaw, that the others cannot see. By asking questions and describing what they have, the students will try, within each group, to discover what the whole picture is. The groups can then compare their relative versions of the final jigsaw.

d) One can also use the *Jigsaw* technique with a set of two similar pictures (e.g. advertising photographs or pictures from magazines). One picture is kept as it is, the second one is cut into pieces, to form a jigsaw puzzle. Students can work in pairs or in small groups and several pictures can be used at the same time.

One group or pair should be given the whole picture; another group of students will get the puzzle and will try to reconstitute the picture by questioning the group who has the whole picture.

e.g. I've got a piece with a hand holding a glass of whisky.

It's in the centre of the picture, a little to the left.

And there's another piece with a wheel on it.

That goes in the bottom left-hand corner, below the piece with the hand and the glass of whisky.

This technique works better with pictures containing a lot of detail. This means the students do not find the solution immediately, and have to ask for further information. It also makes for more interesting dialogue between them.

e) *Tangram*

The Chinese tangram puzzle can be effectively used in similar ways. This puzzle consists of several straight-edged pieces of different dimensions which can be fitted together to form a great variety of patterns. These pieces can easily be made out of stiff paper. Each group (of three) is given a set of tangram pieces and asked to

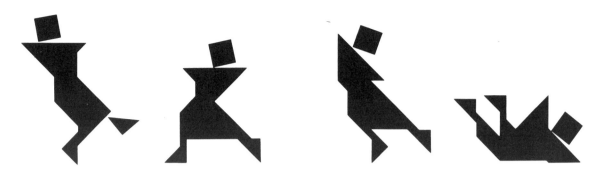

construct a particular pattern (which may be either drawn on the board or circulated as a photocopy). Further developments are described in 14, *Copying*.

14 Copying

The principle of this technique is to follow instructions, oral or written, in order to copy a picture, pattern, or figure.

Choice of pictures

Pictures should be simple, containing a minimum of detail.
Tangram and similar geometric pieces are often used.
Abstract patterns, 'Rorschach' blots, etc. are also suitable.

What to do

a) *Tangram*
    Using the pieces described in 13, *Jigsaws* ask each group to construct its own pattern, abstract or figurative, using *all* the pieces. They should be advised to stick to simple patterns at first. Once the pattern has been made, they must write down the instructions for how to make it. The pieces are then jumbled, and another group is handed the instructions. They must reassemble the figure.

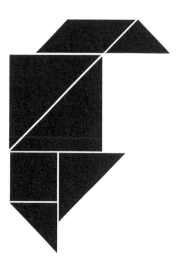

Specimen instructions

First put the two big triangles together to make a square. Then put the parallelogram on top of the square slanting to the right and with one corner on the top left-hand corner of the square. Then take one of the two small triangles and put it into the space between the parallelogram and the top of the square. Now take the small square and put it against the bottom of the larger square you have just made at the left-hand side. Then take the bigger of the two remaining triangles and put it into the right angle formed by the small square and the big square. Then take the last triangle and fit it underneath the small square.

b) *'Telephoned' instructions*

This exercise should be done in pairs, with the two partners seated back-to-back. One is given a simple sketch map or diagram. He then gets his partner to 'copy' this diagram by giving him oral instructions, but without turning round. This requires clear diction and a clear mind!

15   Minimal differences

This is a technique that mainly involves the notion of comparison.

Choice of pictures

Clearly, the pictures chosen should be as similar as possible. Portraits of the same person in different moods or positions, photographs of the same place at different times of day or seasons of the year, pictures of objects that look alike and pictures of the same object from different angles, are all suitable. Likewise, sequences of similar objects (e.g. windows, feet, shoes, etc.) can be used to great effect.

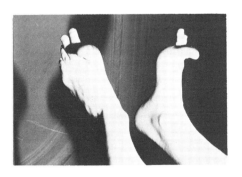

What to do

This technique is particularly suitable for use with the slide projector, since it is then possible to make rapid comparison between pictures. Using pictures (rather than slides) one can choose any of the approaches already described in 4, *Speculation*.

A word, however, should be said about the use of sequences, such as a set of pictures of windows. The purpose of the exercise is not merely to compare the windows but to follow up the associations that each arouses. That is, one is not looking only for descriptive comparison on the lines of: 'This one's wider ... this one's got curtains ... this one has three panes on each side ...' etc. These details will, of course, be noted and mentioned, but there is more to be considered (e.g. 'Who lives behind the window?' 'How often is it opened?' 'What does it look on to?' 'What kind of room lies behind it?' etc.). One can also return to the portraits here, and ask the students to suggest who they think lives behind each window, and why. In brief, with almost any series of objects one is interested in the world that surrounds them, the people that touch, use, or come into contact with them.

16 Passing on the picture

This technique has already been partly described in technique 10, *Finding the words*.

Choice of pictures

No restrictions.

What to do

a) Whatever form the exercise may take, the purpose of *Passing on the picture* remains the same: to permit comparison and discussion, and, most important, to show how differently people can react to the same picture. If any benefit is to be drawn from this, it is important that the picture should not circulate 'unescorted', i.e. there should always be someone who is able to convey to a group what has been said about the same picture in other groups, or else, as in the written exercises, there should be a pooling of the different impressions at the end.

b) An interesting, though challenging, experiment is to ask the group to transmit a picture verbally. The picture is shown briefly to one person only. He then describes it as accurately as possible to his neighbour without anyone else hearing. The description is then passed on down the line. The last person then tells the group what he thinks the picture is like. This is then compared with the picture. The evident weakness of this technique is that no more than two people are involved at a time. One way of countering this is to stagger the process, i.e. when one picture has reached the third person in the group, another picture is passed in the same direction. In this way, more people are involved.

So much, then, for the techniques. To end with, we would only repeat that they should not be considered as *the* techniques, but rather as *some* techniques.

Types of picture

1 Portraits

We have called these 'portraits' for convenience, but it would be better to think of them simply as 'pictures of people'.

Whenever we look at people we, often unconsciously, make assumptions about how they are likely to speak and behave. These assumptions are based first on what we *see*, on details such as clothes, hair, shape of hands, eyes, teeth, etc. As soon as the person speaks, we begin to modify our impressions; and if what he or she says does not 'fit the picture', we feel puzzled, even shocked. Part of the late Groucho Marx's success is that his language belies his appearance: he can dress in a dinner-jacket and be accepted as a 'respectable citizen' – until he opens his mouth!

If you wish to test for yourself the strength of the assumptions we make with our eyes, you need only take a simple phrase, e.g. 'That's very kind of you', 'Get the hell out of here!' and try to imagine it being said in turn by *each* of the people whose pictures follow. You will soon find that with some the words will fit, while with others they will seem most inappropriate.

In many of the exercises we suggest imagining the language that some of these people might use. It is important, then, to make them speak in character.

It is also important to remember that people have affinities and dislikes for others. Many of the exercises in other sections will involve the use of these portraits. The students should imagine how each person would *really* react towards others.

1.1 Main picture (Student's book p. 6)

This picture could be used with techniques 5, *Linking pictures*;   9, *Who am I?*;   10, *Finding the words*;   16, *Passing on the picture*.

REMARKS

1.2 See technique 10, *Finding the words*.

1.3 This picture could be well used with technique 5, *Linking pictures*.

1.4–1.7 See technique 9, *Who am I?* for more detailed comment.

2 Objects

Objects make extremely interesting pictures because, static as they are, they reveal a great deal about their owners and the atmosphere of the place in which they are found.

The suggestions in this section tend not towards a description of the objects themselves but of their surroundings, of the way they are used, of the people one imagines with them, of their past and their future. This is not to say one should leave out all the details in the picture to concentrate exclusively on what it suggests as a whole. On the contrary. A chip, a scratch, a tear or a shiny surface revealing wear or age might indicate a lot about the 'life' of the object.

2.1   Main picture (Student's Book p. 12)

This picture could be used with techniques 1, *Guessing the picture*;   4, *Speculation*;   5, *Linking pictures*;   8, *Blurred focus* (slides only);   10, *Finding the words*.

REMARKS

During the preliminary discussion within the groups, students will clearly need to use sentences expressing opinions and degrees of probability.
e.g. I think it must be something to do with stage props.
    I suppose it's in an old hotel with no running water.
    Couldn't it be a new idea to stop wasting water?
    It might be an exhibit in a museum.
When describing the scene and answering questions, students will be led to use positional adverbs.
e.g. There's a towel next to it on the left.
    In front of the table, a little to the left, a woman wearing a long dress is asleep in
      a wooden chair.

3   People

In this section, you will find pictures of people. Not pictures of their faces only, though, but pictures of people involved with other people or just next to other people, in a situation which tells us something about their daily lives, their occupations, their habits and most of all their own selves.

The common point between these pictures is that they show people's natural reactions to their environment. Even when these photographs are purely anecdotal, they still show that according to their personalities, people behave differently in a certain situation. After a long day's work, for instance, one's reaction can be tiredness, boredom or even violence. Seeing people's attitudes at a given moment may give us an insight into how they might behave in other situations. If we see them at the office, for instance, or travelling to work or on holiday, we may have an idea of what they would be like at home.

It is also interesting to study the setting carefully. Some people seem to belong to their environment; others, on the contrary, seem out of keeping with their surroundings. Ask the students why that is. You may find it useful to get them to look at other pictures in this book and see if and when it would be possible to replace one of the people photographed in this section by someone else. How would it affect the situation? This should help the students define more clearly some of the characteristics of the people in the photographs.

3.1   Main picture (Student's Book p. 18)

This picture, and the others in the section, could be used with techniques 1, *Guessing the picture*;   2, *Reconstructing the picture*;   4, *Speculation*;   5, *Linking pictures*;   8, *Blurred focus*;   10, *Finding the words*.

REMARKS

Thinking about the points in the first question on p. 19 will help the students to imagine these two people outside the surroundings in which they appear here. Set a time limit for doing this (no more than ten minutes) and then ask the students to change partners and to explain briefly what they think to their new partners.

Once they have done the second question, follow the same procedure, adding pictures from the rest of this section, one at a time. Each time a new picture is added, the groups should work out how it relates to the story they have invented so far. In some cases this will be quite easy; in others, it will prove more difficult. But it will create a spirit of competition in the class and the students will want to know how a given group can possibly integrate the new picture to the strange or unexpected story they had invented.

4 Outside

People in the street are usually 'in transit' – neither at home nor at work, but going somewhere, on their way to do something or returning from doing something. This means that whatever may happen to them on the way will usually be accidental, and their reactions will tend to be spontaneous rather than calculated.

In looking at street scenes, therefore, one should concentrate particularly on the gestures and facial expressions of the people involved. Much will be revealed about their present feelings and state of mind. One should also make the effort to imagine the whole context, of which we see only a part. Reactions in a busy street, for instance, will be different from reactions in a village lane. The presence of other people (How many?) is important.

Physical details, too, are revealing. Cracks in the pavement, torn posters, well-painted shop-fronts, litter in the gutter, etc. can give indications about the environment. And people's clothes may often seem to be out-of-keeping with the surroundings they are in. Weather also influences behaviour in the street. A quick look at the way people are dressed will tell you, roughly, how warm or cold it is.

One should try to avoid making snap judgements. The fact that a street may be 'identifiable' as a London, Paris or New York street, should not necessarily influence conclusions about what the people are doing in this street. Hence the importance of deciding whether or not these people fit into their surroundings. In thinking about these pictures, it may occasionally be helpful for students to ask themselves who the photographer might have been, where he or she was standing, and, most important, why the picture was taken.

4.1 Main picture (Student's Book p. 24)

This picture could be used with techniques 4, *Speculation*;   5, *Linking pictures*;   9, *Who am I?*;   10, *Finding the words*;   13, *Jigsaws*.
See also the introduction and technique 5, *Linking pictures,* for question 2.

REMARKS

4.2   This picture would also be suitable for technique 2, *Reconstructing the picture.*

4.3   A variant of technique 5, *Linking pictures,* is used here.

5 Atmosphere

A picture of a young girl all in white, holding a parasol and staring reflectively into a lily-pond may appear to one observer as 'Memories of childhood' and to another as, simply, 'Girl looking at goldfish'. Atmosphere is as much in the eye of the observer as it is in the picture.

The pictures in this section have been grouped under *Atmosphere* not because they were necessarily intended to be 'atmospheric' but because they struck us as being suggestive.

Picture 5.2, for instance, of a man in a deckchair is, if you like, just a picture from a seaside resort. But as soon as we begin to interest ourselves in who the man is and, particularly, who took the picture, we find that it begins to open up. The more we know of the background, the greater our interest is likely to be.

If we are to allow ourselves to be affected by a picture we need to be able to think beyond the frame to people and objects not visible here. To return to the man in the deckchair: how different his reading the paper on the beach would seem if we supposed that this were the first holiday he had ever had at the sea, if we imagined that his car was at this moment being stolen, if we considered that he might be in disguise, etc.

What we are trying to do here is not impose our atmosphere on the picture, but let the picture suggest what it will.

5.1 Main picture (Student's Book p. 30)

This picture could be used with techniques 4, *Speculation*;   5, *Linking pictures*;   9, *Who am I?*;   10, *Finding the words*;   13, *Jigsaws*.

REMARKS

5.2, 5.3 See also the introduction and technique 5, *Linking pictures*.

6 Images

The pictures in this section are not necessarily advertisements, indeed, very few of them are. But they are pictures we felt might easily have been used in advertising or publicity.

The technique that can always be used to great effect with such pictures is 10, *Finding the words*. Since the impact of a good advertisement lies not in an obvious relation between words and picture, but in an unexpected or unpredictable connection, free play can be given to the imagination here. It should not be forgotten, however, that most of these pictures can be used with other techniques as well.

If you are interested in looking for your own material you might begin by browsing round a book or record shop in order to see what kind of pictures are in fact used for this kind of publicity, taking note of features such as colour, focus (Is blurred focus often used? If so, for what effect?), the use of abstract designs and collages, etc. After this, it will be easier to select pictures that might belong in this section.

6.1   Main picture (Student's Book p. 36)

This picture could be used with techniques 1, *Guessing the picture*;   5, *Linking pictures*;   8, *Blurred focus*;   9, *Who am I?*;   10, *Finding the words*.

REMARKS

6.2   This picture would also be extremely suitable for techniques 1, *Guessing the picture* and 5, *Linking pictures*.

6.3   Use technique 1, *Guessing the picture*, and insist on getting the *exact* wording of the notice.

7   Mystery

Pictures can be mysterious in many different ways. In some cases we cannot decide exactly what the picture is about. In others we can see what is happening but cannot find an easy explanation for it. In others again it is the unusual combination of objects and people, or expressions which gives the air of something strange and unexplained. And in some rare cases the picture seems to be now one thing, now another.

In all cases, when dealing with pictures of this kind, it is advisable to spend time on examining *all* the possible interpretations and not letting students jump immediately to the most obvious or most appealing one.

7.1   Main picture (Student's Book p. 42)

This picture could be used with techniques 1, *Guessing the picture*;   4, *Speculation*;   5, *Linking pictures*;   8, *Blurred focus*;   10, *Finding the words*;   13, *Jigsaws*;   14, *Copying*;   15, *Minimal differences* (see picture 7.1, p. 42);   16, *Passing on the picture*.

REMARKS

It may be helpful to remind students of the different ways of expressing degrees of probability before they start work.
e.g. Probably . . .
    Maybe . . .
    It looks as if . . .
    It might be . . .
    It could be . . .
    I suppose . . .

8   A different view

The pictures in this section have one point in common: it is not immediately clear to the eye what they represent. This may come from the subject itself which is uncommon or strange, from the angle which is unusual, or from the technique of the photographer (close-ups, use of filters, high-speed shots, etc.).

When working on these pictures, what matters is not so much finding out the 'solution', discovering what the picture actually *is*, but rather, opening oneself to all kinds of possibilities, realising that it may have multiple meanings.

Technique 4, *Speculation* will always be a basic technique when dealing with these pictures. 5, *Linking pictures* will also be particularly interesting. By forcing the students to integrate the picture in a story this technique will bring out its potential interpretations. Most of these pictures lend themselves particularly well to the writing of short poems, articles or advertising slogans.

8.1   Main picture (Student's Book p. 48)

This picture can be used with techniques 1, *Guessing the picture*;   4, *Speculation*;   5, *Linking pictures*;   10, *Finding the words*.

9   Collages

Collages offer us a relatively simple way of associating objects, colours, parts of the body, etc. in attractive and often unexpected ways.

Apart from their intrinsic attraction, as objects to look at, they tend to spark off unusual associations of ideas, and this is what makes them so useful for language work.

9.1   Main picture (Student's Book p. 54)

This picture could be used with techniques 4, *Speculation*;   5, *Linking pictures*;   10, *Finding the words*.

REMARKS

Students can make their own collages as group projects. It is advisable to give them some guidelines (e.g. Use only one geometrical shape; use only three colours; use only wheels, etc. Or give them a key-word, e.g. starvation).
Groups then present their collages to each other.

10   Surrealism

The surrealistic painters tried by their unusual way of looking at people and objects, and by unexpected juxtapositions, combinations and transformations, to jog people out of their accustomed ways of seeing, to make them re-assess the nature of reality. They very often drew on the imagery of the subconscious and of dreams to achieve this.

Pictures of this kind are peculiarly powerful in stimulating the imagination and provoking interesting responses. Not everyone sees, or interprets what he sees in these pictures in the same way. That is the main reason for including them here.

The suggestions made here by no means exhaust the possibilities of pictures of this type.

Apart from Martin Escher and René Magritte, the work of Giorgio de Chirico, Max Ernst and Salvador Dalí abounds in pictures of this kind.

10.1 Main picture (Student's Book p. 60)

This picture could be used with techniques 1, *Guessing the picture*;   3, *You're a witness*;   4, *Speculation*;   5, *Linking pictures*;   8, *Blurred focus*;   10, *Finding the words*;   14, *Copying*;   15, *Minimal differences*.

REMARKS

After the students have done the second question, use the ideas generated in this exchange session to have a general class discussion.

11 Sequences

When we see a series of pictures which tell a story they are normally presented in the order in which the story happened. Here, they will be mixed up, out of order, and the main task is, through discussion, to put them into an acceptable order again.

Sometimes the order may seem obvious, at others it is much more difficult to work out and needs a real effort to interpret. But even in apparently 'obvious' sequences there may be alternative ways of ordering the pictures.

REMARKS

The ideal way of using a sequence of this kind is to have the pictures on separate pieces of card. (It is easy to prepare sets of these.) Each group then receives a different picture. The group which thinks it has the first picture in the sequence then describes it to the rest. A group which thinks it has a picture which might follow it then contributes its description and so on. This affords considerable opportunity for clarification and cross-questioning between groups.

11.1 Main picture (Student's Book p. 68)

11.2 In this sequence *hands* are used. It is relatively easy to make up sequences involving feet (see p. 27), eyes, lips, etc. which are likewise expressive of moods, feelings, actions, etc.

12 Cartoons

In this section, you will find single, unrelated cartoons. They can be used with many of the techniques mentioned and are often very close to the pictures in section 3, *People*. However, many cartoons tend to exaggerate certain features and to explain what is often not very clear in a picture. This is the case of the drawing by Sempé, the main picture in the section. With such drawings, it is interesting to imagine the events that might have led to this particular situation as well as what will happen later. Other drawings on the contrary, are much more open and appeal to one's imagination and fancy. One might first try to find some common points between the drawings, and discuss them with the class as a whole. Students can then try to match these drawings with the thoughts or dreams of some of the people whose portraits can be found in the book.

12.1 Main picture (Student's Book p. 74)

This picture could be used with techniques 1, *Guessing the picture*; 4, *Speculation*; 6, *Linking cartoons*; 8, *Blurred focus*; 10, *Finding the words*.

13 Split cartoons

See technique 12, *Split cartoons* (p. 22) for a detailed description. Although this technique is best handled using slides or flash cards, the examples given in this section will show that, even when you have all the elements under your eyes, several interpretations are still possible.

13.1 Main picture (Student's Book p. 80)

REMARKS

Another possibility is for each group to go to another group and ask each other questions to find out how they have 'built' their picture.

14 Minimal differences

With minimal differences, it is important that the pictures used should be as similar as possible. For this reason, it is a section which offers great scope for 'do-it-yourself' work. Those interested in extending the ideas we have suggested here might try the following:
– Ask students to photograph a particular street, shop, building, or road at different times of day, which they should note. This will provide interesting material in which one element (the static one) will be constant, although the surrounding context may have changed.
– Ask students to photograph sets of similar objects. (In the Student's Book feet and windows are used.) Other suitable subjects would be hands, hats, signposts and notices,* posters, street-lights, bodies lying down (e.g. on beaches, benches, lawns, etc.), people seen from behind, staircases, door-handles, chimneys, large clocks on public buildings, etc.
– Ask students to collect pictures from different magazines in which the same object (e.g. a milk bottle, a pound note, a tennis racquet, a typewriter) appears.

14.1 Main picture (Student's Book p. 84)

These pictures could be used with techniques 2, *Reconstructing the picture*; 3, *You're a witness*; 4, *Speculation*; 5, *Linking pictures*; 7, *Finding the last picture*; 10, *Finding the words*; 11, *Ordering a sequence*; 15, *Minimal differences*.

After the students have done question 3, you may like to set up a panel to select which scenario would be the best to use.

* See Alan Duff: *That's Life!* (Cambridge University Press) for a series of photographs of public notices and signs.

REMARKS

14.4 Question 2 can also be done using loose portraits pinned to the wall or circulated among the groups. Each picture should be numbered.

Instead of pictures of people, a tape recording of voices can also be used. In this case, it is the *voice* rather than the body which must be matched with the feet.

14.4—14.12 These photographs consist of a series of related pictures: feet of different types, in different kinds of positions and windows of all sorts. These pictures can obviously be used with technique 15, *Minimal differences,* but it is mainly the fact of comparing things one usually thinks of as roughly similar that will be interesting. Even if some of the windows, for instance, look almost alike at first sight, a closer look will reveal that a window-pane is cracked, or one of the curtains is dirty, or that you can have a glimpse of something going on inside . . . and this will change completely one's vision of the picture.

Students should ask themselves about the people who live behind a window (e.g. Why didn't they repair it? Are they too poor, or just too busy? Don't they care? Or is it because nobody lives there any longer? And if so, why?) A further step might be to match each of the windows with a character in the book.

14.13—14.17 For each of these pictures students should work in pairs. A will look at the pictures in this section, B will need to look elsewhere in the book as indicated. It is important that A and B do not see each others' pictures.

Student A	*Student B*	
14.13	1.6	(p. 11)
14.14	8.3	(p. 51)
14.15	6.5	(p. 40)
14.16	7.1	(p. 42)
14.17	10.9	(p. 66)

The partners should exchange information about their pictures so as to find out what differences there are between them. This will involve asking questions and taking careful notes. When they have finished, they should look at the two pictures together and check the accuracy of their notes.

15 Illusions

In this section we have taken advantage of the fact that the same visual 'facts' may be 'seen' differently by different people. The eye sees a pattern of shapes and colours. The brain organises this raw visual material into comprehensible patterns.

Different people often organise identical phenomena differently and will tell us they 'see' different things from others. Even a single person may look at the same picture and 'see' now one thing, now another. This fact clearly gives considerable scope for discussion.

Here are some suggestions for work involving optical illusions in addition to those in the Student's Book.

Without showing anyone else what they are doing, ask students to complete the pictures below in any way they like.

When they have finished, they should compare their results with two other people. Are there any similarities or differences? Do some people always tend to draw certain kinds of things?

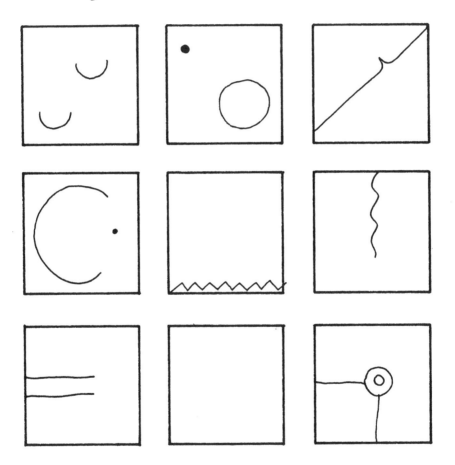

INK BLOTS

Ask students to make their own ink blots or look at the following pictures. They should work in pairs. Ask them what they can see, what sense they can make of them, to write down all their ideas, and to compare them with another pair. Here are some hints:
– Look at the picture 'upside down' and 'sideways' as well as the 'right way up'.
– Look at the shapes made by the black parts. Then focus on the shapes made by the white parts.

– Look at them with 'blurred' vision so that you can just see the vague, overall shape. A follow-up exercise to this is to do the same exercise with pictures of clouds or shadows.

REAL OPTICAL ILLUSIONS

Students should look carefully at this picture in pairs. There are a number of things 'wrong' with it. They could not possibly be like that in real life. They should see how many they can find, then compare notes with another pair.

Which of these men is the tallest? Students should discuss their answers in pairs. Ask if they know of any other pictures like this.

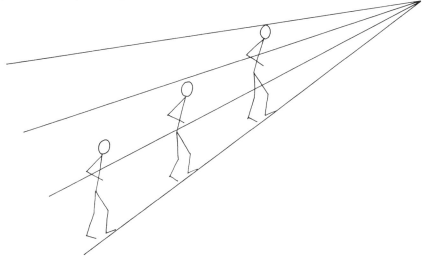

BLIND DRAWING

Ask students to draw these pictures without looking at their own piece of paper and hand at all.

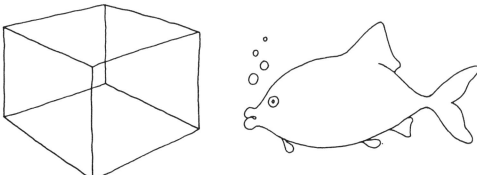

When they have finished, they compare results with a partner.

Then work in pairs. This time A has a drawing, B has the paper and pencil. A must give instructions to B on how to make the drawing. A may not look at the paper he is drawing on.

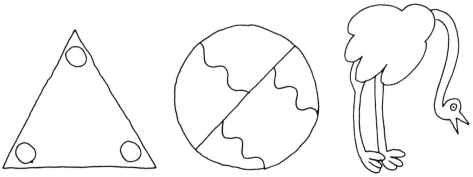

VISUAL CONSEQUENCES

For this students should be in groups *of exactly five people*. Each person needs a piece of paper and a pen or pencil.

At the top of the paper everyone draws a head and neck (it may be human, animal or fantastic). The papers are then folded so that the head is not visible, and passed on to the next person in the group. Everyone then draws the top half of the creature (with arms, wings, etc.). Papers are then passed on again. The same procedure is followed for the body, legs and feet.

At the end everyone unfolds his paper and compares it with those of the others in the group.

Ask students to choose a name, or title for each of the 'creatures', and then make up stories in which all five creatures are involved.

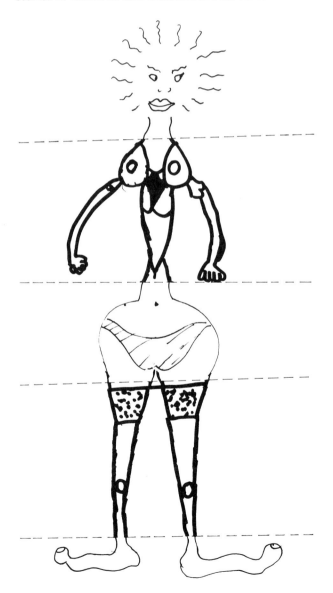